Mississippi Bingo Book

COMPLETE BINGO GAME IN A BOOK

THE GREAT SEAL OF THE STATE OF MISSISSIPPI

IN GOD WE TRUST

Written By Rebecca Stark

Educational Books 'n' Bingo

ISBN 978-0-87386-517-3

Printed in the U.S.A.

DIRECTIONS

INCLUDED:

List of Terms

Templates for Additional Terms and Clues

2 Clues per Term

30 Unique Bingo Cards

Markers

1. **Either cut apart the book or make copies of ALL the sheets. You might want to make an extra copy of the clue sheets to use for introduction and review. Keep the sheets in an envelope for easy reuse.**

2. Cut apart the call cards with terms and clues.

3. Pass out one bingo card per student. There are enough for a class of 30.

4. Pass out markers. You may cut apart the markers included in this book or use any other small items of your choice.

5. Decide whether or not you will require the entire card to be filled. Requiring the entire card to be filled provides a better review. However, if you have a short time to fill, you may prefer to have them do the just the border or some other format. Tell the class before you begin what is required.

6. There are 50 terms. Read the list before you begin. If there are any terms that have not been covered in class, you may want to read to the students the term and clues before you begin.

7. There is a blank space in the middle of each card. You can instruct the students to use it as a free space or you can write in answers to cover terms not included. Of course, in this case you would create your own clues. (Templates provided.)

8. Shuffle the cards and place them in a pile. Two or three clues are provided for each term. If you plan to play the game with the same group more than once, you might want to choose a different clue for each game. If not, you may choose to use more than one clue.

9. Be sure to keep the cards you have used for the present game in a separate pile. When a student calls, "Bingo," he or she will have to verify that the correct answers are on his or her card AND that the markers were placed in response to the proper questions. Pull out the cards that are on the student's card keeping them in the order they were used in the game. Read each clue as it was given and ask the student to identify the correct answer from his or her card.

10. If the student has the correct answers on the card AND has shown that they were marked in response to the *correct questions*, then that student is the winner and the game is over. If the student does not have the correct answers on the card OR he or she marked the answers in response to *the wrong questions*, then the game continues until there is a proper winner.

11. If you want to play again, reshuffle the cards and begin again.

Have fun!

TERMS INCLUDED

Agricultural

Alligator(s)

Antebellum

Basilosaurus

Border(s)

Bottlenose Dolphin

Civil War

William C. Claiborne

Climate

Confederate States of America

Cotton

County (-ies)

Jefferson Davis

Hernando de Soto

Elvis

Medgar Evers

Executive Branch

Fishing

France/French

Freedmen

Gulfport

Honeybee

Industry (-ies)

Jackson

Judicial Branch

Katrina

Legislative Branch

Magnolia

Milk

Mississippi Delta

Mississippi River

Mockingbird(s)

Motto

Natchez

Native American

Petrified Wood

John J. Pettus

Pinckney's Treaty of 1795

Plantation(s)

Sharecropping (-er)

State Song

Territory

Treaty of Paris of 1763

Tupelo

Union

University of Mississippi

Vicksburg

White-tail Deer

Oprah Winfrey

Woodall Mountain

Mississippi Bingo

Additional Terms

Choose as many additional terms as you would like and write them in the squares. Repeat each as desired.
Cut out the squares and randomly distribute them to the class.
Instruct the students to place their square on the center space of their card.

Clues for Additional Terms

Write three clues for each of your additional terms.

_____ 1. 2. 3.	_____ 1. 2. 3.
_____ 1. 2. 3.	_____ 1. 2. 3.
_____ 1. 2. 3.	_____ 1. 2. 3.

© Barbara M. Peller

Agricultural 1. The most important ___ products are broilers; cotton; soybeans; farm-raised catfish; and cattle and calves. 2. The production of cotton accounts for about 13% of the state's total ___ receipts.	**Alligator(s)** 1. The American ___ is the state reptile. 2. American ___ are usually found in freshwater swamps, marshes, rivers, and lakes.
Antebellum 1. ___ means "existing before a war," especially before the American Civil War. 2. Many tourists visit Natchez to tour the ___ plantations and other historic sites.	**Basilosaurus** 1. ___ is the official state fossil. 2. ___ is an extinct primitive whale. It and other primitive whales have been found in Louisiana, Mississippi, and Alabama.
Border(s) 1. These states ___ Mississippi: Alabama, Arkansas, Louisiana, and Tennessee. 2. The Gulf of Mexico ___ Mississippi to the south.	**Bottlenose Dolphin** 1. The ___ is the state water mammal. 2. The ___ uses SONAR to echolocate fish.
Civil War 1. Mississippi's location along the Mississippi River made it strategically important to both the North and South during the ___. 2. Slavery and states' rights were important issues that led to the American ___.	**William C. Claiborne** 1. ___ was governor and superintendent of Indian affairs in the Mississippi Territory from 1801 through 1803. 2. As superintendent of Indian affairs, ___ worked to work out differences with the Choctaw and Chicasaw and to improve the well-being of the Native Americans.
Climate 1. Mississippi has a humid, sub-tropical ___. 2. A humid, sub-tropical ___ is characterized by hot, humid summers and generally mild to cool winters.	**Confederate States of America** 1. The ___ was a government set up from 1861 to 1865. 2. In February 1861, Mississippi joined with six other states to form the Confederate States of America. Four other states later joined.
Mississippi Bingo	© Barbara M. Peller

Cotton	**County (-ies)**
1. The ___ gin was invented by Eli Whitney in the late 18th century. 2. Only Texas exceeds Mississippi in the production of ___.	1. Mississippi has 82 ___. 2. Hinds is the largest ___. Jackson and Raymond are its two ___ seats.
Jefferson Davis	**Hernando de Soto**
1. He was president of the Confederacy. 2. Before becoming President of the Confederacy, ___ was a U.S. senator from Mississippi.	1. Mississippi was first explored for Territory by ___. 2. ___ became the first European to discover the Mississippi River in 1540.
Elvis (Presley)	**Medgar Evers**
1. He was born in Tupelo, Mississippi. 2. His birthplace is now a historic museum site in Tupelo, Mississippi.	1. ___ was an African American civil rights activist. 2. ___ was assassinated in Jackson, Mississippi, in 1963. In 1969, his brother Charles became the first black man elected mayor in the state.
Executive Branch	**Fishing**
1. The governor is head of the ___. The present-day governor is [fill in]. 2. The ___ of government enforces laws. It includes the governor, the lieutenant governor, the attorney general, the secretary of state, the state auditor, and the treasurer.	1. Commercial ___, especially shellfish, is an important industry. Mississippi is a leading shrimp-producing state. 2. Some important products of the ___ industry include shrimp, oysters, catfish, and menhaden.
France/French	**Freedmen**
1. From 1699 to 1763, the future state of Mississippi was a part of the ___ colony of Louisiana. 2. In the 1763 Treaty of Paris, ___ gave its holdings east of the Mississippi to England.	1. ___ are former slaves who were released from slavery by legal means. 2. The ___'s Bureau was a federal agency that aided former slaves during Reconstruction.

Mississippi Bingo

Gulfport	**Honeybee**
1. ___ is the second largest city in the state. 2. ___ is the co-county seat with Biloxi of Harrison County.	1. The ___ was designated the state Insect of Mississippi in 1980. 2. The ___ is official state symbol in 17 states, probably because they play an important role in agriculture.
Industry (-ies)	**Jackson**
1. Agriculture is still the most important ___. 2. Important ___ include food processing, meatpacking, and furniture production.	1. ___ is the state capital and the largest city in the state. 2. ___ was named for the man who would become the seventh President of the United States.
Judicial Branch	**Katrina**
1. The ___ interprets what our laws mean and makes decisions about the laws and those who break them. 2. The ___ is made up of several courts, the highest of which is the state Supreme Court.	1. Hurricane ___ was a deadly storm of the 2005 Atlantic hurricane season. 2. At least 1,836 people died as a result of Hurricane ___ and the floods that followed.
Legislative Branch	**Magnolia**
1. The ___ branch of government comprises the State Senate and the House of Representatives. 2. The ___ makes the laws.	1. Mississippi is often called "The ___ State." 2. The ___ is the state tree. It is also the state flower, which is pictured on the state quarter.
Milk	**Mississippi Delta**
1. ___ is the state beverage. 2. ___ has been called a nearly perfect food. It is a source of protein, calcium, and several other important nutrients.	1. The area known as the ___ lies between the Mississippi and Yazoo rivers. 2. The ___ is in the northwestern part of Mississippi. This fertile region is one of the richest cotton-growing areas.

Mississippi Bingo

Mississippi River 1. The ___ forms the entire western border of the state. 2.The ___, the Big Black River, the Pearl River, and the Yazoo River are important rivers in Mississippi.	**Mockingbird(s)** 1. The ___ is the state bird. 2. ___ often mimic the songs and sounds of other creatures.
Motto 1. The ___ *"Virtute et armis"* is on the state coat of arms. 2. The translation of the Latin ___ *"Virtute et armis"* is "By valor and arms."	**Natchez** 1. ___ was the first state capital. It is located on the Mississippi River. 2. ___ is named for the tribe of Native Americans who lived in the vicinity when the Europeans arrived.
Native American 1. Most ___ were forced to leave Mississippi during the Indian Removals of the 1800s. 2. The Mississippi Band of Choctaw Indians is the only federally recognized ___ tribe in Mississippi today.	**Petrified Wood** 1. ___ is the state stone. The Mississippi ___ Forest is in Flora, Mississippi. 2. ___ is actually a fossil.
John J. Pettus 1. ___ was governor when Mississippi seceded in 1861. 2. He was the twentieth and the twenty-third governor of Mississippi. His first term lasted only five days.	**Pinckney's Treaty of 1795** 1. ___, also called the Treaty of San Lorenzo, put the lands of the Chickasaw and Choctaw Nations within the new boundaries of the United States. 2. ___ ended Spanish control of Mississippi.
Plantation(s) 1. A ___ is a large agricultural estate where crops are grown for sale. It is usually worked by resident labor. 2. Mississippi had many sprawling cotton ___ with magnificent homes. Many antebellum mansions were lost during the Civil War, but some remain.	**Sharecropping (-er)** 1. ___ is a system of agriculture in which a landowner allows a tenant to use the land in return for a share of the crop produced. 2. A ___ is a tenant farmer who gives a share of the crops raised to the landlord in place of rent.

State Song 1. "Go, Mississippi" is the official ___. It was written by William Houston Davis. 2. The first line of the ___ is "States may sing their songs of praise."	**Territory** 1. Mississippi ___ originally included Misssissippi and Alabama. 2. The Mississippi___ was organized in 1798 from land that had been disputed by the U.S. and Spain. The extreme southern part of the state, which had been part of West Florida, was annexed in 1812.
Treaty of Paris of 1763 1. The ___ officially ended the French and Indian War between the British and the French. 2. As part of the ___, France gave up all its holdings east of the Mississippi to England.	**Tupelo** 1. ___ is known as the birthplace of Elvis Presley. 2. ___ has one of the largest automobile museums in North America.
Union 1. Mississippi was admitted to the ___ as the 20th state on December 10, 1817. 2. Mississippi was the second state to secede from the ___. Eventually 11 states seceded.	**University of Mississippi** 1. The ___ is affectionately called Ole Mis. 2. This public research university in Oxford, Mississippi, was founded in 1844.
Vicksburg 1. ___ was the most important Confederate stronghold on the Mississippi River. Its surrender and the defeat at Gettysburg are often called the turning points of the Civil War. 2. After the surrender of Vicksburg, the Union Army gained control of the Mississippi River.	**White-tail Deer** 1. The ___ and the red fox are the state land mammals. 2. ___ can run up to 40 miles per hour and swim 13 miles per hour. The white underside of the its tail waves when running and is flashed as a danger signal.
Oprah Winfrey 1. This media mogul, talk show host, actress, producer, and philanthropist was born in Kosciusko, Mississippi, in 1954. 2. Born into poverty in rural Mississippi, she is now one of the richest and most influential people in the world!	**Woodall Mountain** 1. At only 806 feet, ___ is the highest point in the state. 2. ___, the highest point in the state, is in the northeast corner of Mississippi.

Mississippi Bingo

Plantation(s)	Agricultural	Antebellum	France/French	Bottlenose Dolphin
Fishing	Alligator(s)	Vicksburg	Mississippi Delta	State Song
University of Mississippi	Mississippi River		Petrified Wood	White-tail Deer
Union	Sharecropping (-er)	Tupelo	Magnolia	Motto
Native American	Honeybee	Hernando de Soto	Treaty of Paris of 1763	Jackson

Mississippi Bingo

Union	University of Mississippi	Industry (-ies)	Milk	Legislative Branch
Motto	Medgar Evers	William C. Claiborne	Sharecropping (-er)	Natchez
Confederate States of America	Honeybee		Hurricane Katrina	Tupelo
John J. Pettus	Pinckney's Treaty of 1795	Mississippi River	Oprah Winfrey	Bottlenose Dolphin
State Song	Vicksburg	Hernando de Soto	Fishing	Treaty of Paris of 1763

Mississippi Bingo: Card No. 2

Mississippi Bingo

Honeybee	Tupelo	Medgar Evers	Magnolia	University of Mississippi
Motto	Alligator(s)	Climate	Agricultural	Gulfport
Sharecropping (-er)	Vicksburg		Natchez	Border(s)
Mississippi River	Confederate States of America	Native American	John J. Pettus	Industry (-ies)
Treaty of Paris of 1763	Cotton	Hernando de Soto	Oprah Winfrey	Legislative Branch

Mississippi Bingo

Mississippi River	Natchez	Antebellum	Cotton	Legislative Branch
Mockingbird(s)	Civil War	Agricultural	Milk	University of Mississippi
Petrified Wood	John J. Pettus		Jackson	France/French
Tupelo	Alligator(s)	Vicksburg	Hernando de Soto	William C. Claiborne
County (-ies)	State Song	Basilosaurus	Treaty of Paris of 1763	White-tail Deer

Mississippi Bingo

State Song	Bottlenose Dolphin	Sharecropping (-er)	William C. Claiborne	Cotton
Mockingbird(s)	Tupelo	Climate	Hurricane Katrina	Alligator(s)
Antebellum	White-tail Deer		Mississippi Delta	Freedmen
Jackson	Legislative Branch	Plantation(s)	Oprah Winfrey	Jefferson Davis
Medgar Evers	Hernando de Soto	University of Mississippi	Mississippi River	Petrified Wood

Mississippi Bingo: Card No. 5

Mississippi Bingo

Border(s)	Natchez	Industry (-ies)	Legislative Branch	White-tail Deer
Magnolia	Sharecropping (-er)	Jefferson Davis	Agricultural	University of Mississippi
Milk	County (-ies)		Civil War	Hurricane Katrina
Hernando de Soto	Native American	Oprah Winfrey	Basilosaurus	Antebellum
Motto	William C. Claiborne	Plantation(s)	Petrified Wood	Executive Branch

Mississippi Bingo

Plantation(s)	Natchez	Freedmen	Tupelo	Medgar Evers
Motto	Legislative Branch	Honeybee	Alligator(s)	Mockingbird(s)
White-tail Deer	France/French		Hurricane Katrina	Civil War
Mississippi River	John J. Pettus	Climate	Union	Confederate States of America
Hernando de Soto	Cotton	Oprah Winfrey	Basilosaurus	Border(s)

Mississippi Bingo

Petrified Wood	Natchez	Elvis	Magnolia	Civil War
Mockingbird(s)	Antebellum	Milk	White-tail Deer	William C. Claiborne
Executive Branch	Cotton		Legislative Branch	Bottlenose Dolphin
Treaty of Paris of 1763	Mississippi River	Union	County (-ies)	John J. Pettus
Vicksburg	Hernando de Soto	Basilosaurus	Sharecropping (-er)	Motto

Mississippi Bingo

Hurricane Katrina	Medgar Evers	Honeybee	Executive Branch	Cotton
County (-ies)	Legislative Branch	Petrified Wood	Sharecropping (-er)	Natchez
Gulfport	Plantation(s)		Alligator(s)	Elvis
Jefferson Davis	Bottlenose Dolphin	Native American	Mississippi Delta	Freedmen
John J. Pettus	Oprah Winfrey	Climate	Union	Jackson

Mississippi Bingo: Card No. 9

Mississippi Bingo

Union	Magnolia	Civil War	Milk	Executive Branch
White-tail Deer	William C. Claiborne	Agricultural	Alligator(s)	Legislative Branch
Cotton	Natchez		France/French	Confederate States of America
Native American	Jackson	Jefferson Davis	Oprah Winfrey	Gulfport
Climate	Motto	Industry (-ies)	State Song	Petrified Wood

Mississippi Bingo

Border(s)	Natchez	Sharecropping (-er)	Jefferson Davis	Motto
Elvis	Gulfport	Mississippi Delta	Hurricane Katrina	Agricultural
Mockingbird(s)	Legislative Branch		Industry (-ies)	Honeybee
Climate	University of Mississippi	Oprah Winfrey	Cotton	Union
County (-ies)	Hernando de Soto	Plantation(s)	Basilosaurus	Medgar Evers

Mississippi Bingo: Card No. 11

Mississippi Bingo

Medgar Evers	Bottlenose Dolphin	Gulfport	Magnolia	Hurricane Katrina
Honeybee	Motto	Antebellum	Basilosaurus	Alligator(s)
Plantation(s)	Freedmen		White-tail Deer	Milk
Hernando de Soto	John J. Pettus	Legislative Branch	Union	Mockingbird(s)
Natchez	Elvis	Cotton	County (-ies)	William C. Claiborne

Mississippi Bingo

Jefferson Davis	Bottlenose Dolphin	Border(s)	Gulfport	White-tail Deer
Antebellum	Elvis	Legislative Branch	Hurricane Katrina	Confederate States of America
Magnolia	William C. Claiborne		Honeybee	Freedmen
Petrified Wood	Oprah Winfrey	Civil War	Cotton	Union
Hernando de Soto	Jackson	Basilosaurus	Plantation(s)	Mississippi Delta

Mississippi Bingo: Card No. 13

Mississippi Bingo

Fishing	Legislative Branch	Sharecropping (-er)	Hurricane Katrina	County (-ies)
William C. Claiborne	Plantation(s)	Gulfport	Alligator(s)	Natchez
Jefferson Davis	France/French		Industry (-ies)	Climate
Jackson	Oprah Winfrey	Cotton	Civil War	Border(s)
Hernando de Soto	Milk	Confederate States of America	Motto	Petrified Wood

Mississippi Bingo

Mississippi Delta	Hurricane Katrina	Sharecropping (-er)	Medgar Evers	Magnolia
Border(s)	Industry (-ies)	Agricultural	Antebellum	County (-ies)
White-tail Deer	Plantation(s)		University of Mississippi	Natchez
Hernando de Soto	Gulfport	Elvis	Oprah Winfrey	Jefferson Davis
Motto	John J. Pettus	Basilosaurus	Executive Branch	Honeybee

Mississippi Bingo: Card No. 15

Mississippi Bingo

Civil War	Gulfport	Elvis	Executive Branch	Pinckney's Treaty of 1795
Milk	Confederate States of America	Freedmen	Mockingbird(s)	France/French
Jefferson Davis	Bottlenose Dolphin		White-tail Deer	Honeybee
Mississippi River	William C. Claiborne	Hernando de Soto	Mississippi Delta	Union
County (-ies)	Woodall Mountain	Basilosaurus	John J. Pettus	Natchez

Mississippi Bingo

Climate	Territory	Judicial Branch	Gulfport	Fishing
Mississippi Delta	County (-ies)	Oprah Winfrey	France/French	Freedmen
Hurricane Katrina	Petrified Wood		Woodall Mountain	Elvis
Jackson	Motto	Union	Sharecropping (-er)	Confederate States of America
Native American	Jefferson Davis	Medgar Evers	Magnolia	Bottlenose Dolphin

Mississippi Bingo

Executive Branch	Cotton	William C. Claiborne	Jefferson Davis	Milk
Natchez	Climate	Native American	White-tail Deer	County (-ies)
Hurricane Katrina	Confederate States of America		Judicial Branch	Antebellum
Bottlenose Dolphin	Agricultural	Oprah Winfrey	Union	Industry (-ies)
Woodall Mountain	Gulfport	Sharecropping (-er)	Territory	Border(s)

Mississippi Bingo

White-tail Deer	Border(s)	Gulfport	Elvis	Union
Mississippi Delta	Magnolia	Natchez	Medgar Evers	France/French
Territory	Cotton		Alligator(s)	University of Mississippi
Industry (-ies)	Woodall Mountain	Native American	John J. Pettus	Judicial Branch
Antebellum	Pinckney's Treaty of 1795	Motto	Petrified Wood	Basilosaurus

Mississippi Bingo

Fishing	Territory	Magnolia	Gulfport	Basilosaurus
William C. Claiborne	Honeybee	Mockingbird(s)	Native American	Milk
Bottlenose Dolphin	Freedmen		Mississippi River	Agricultural
State Song	Vicksburg	Treaty of Paris of 1763	John J. Pettus	Woodall Mountain
Tupelo	Petrified Wood	Pinckney's Treaty of 1795	Union	Judicial Branch

Mississippi Bingo

Mississippi Delta	Border(s)	Mockingbird(s)	Gulfport	State Song
Bottlenose Dolphin	Judicial Branch	Civil War	Elvis	Plantation(s)
Confederate States of America	Motto		Territory	Sharecropping (-er)
Native American	Medgar Evers	Woodall Mountain	Jackson	Petrified Wood
Mississippi River	Pinckney's Treaty of 1795	Basilosaurus	Climate	John J. Pettus

Mississippi Bingo

Executive Branch	Industry (-ies)	Judicial Branch	Antebellum	Jefferson Davis
Milk	Magnolia	University of Mississippi	Elvis	Alligator(s)
William C. Claiborne	France/French		Plantation(s)	Freedmen
Woodall Mountain	Jackson	John J. Pettus	Agricultural	Mockingbird(s)
Pinckney's Treaty of 1795	Climate	Territory	Confederate States of America	Mississippi River

Mississippi Bingo

Civil War	Territory	Medgar Evers	Antebellum	Basilosaurus
Border(s)	Fishing	Motto	Mississippi Delta	Agricultural
Industry (-ies)	Jefferson Davis		Treaty of Paris of 1763	Plantation(s)
Confederate States of America	Pinckney's Treaty of 1795	Woodall Mountain	Climate	John J. Pettus
State Song	Vicksburg	Petrified Wood	Native American	Judicial Branch

Mississippi Bingo

Civil War	Petrified Wood	Fishing	Territory	Elvis
Judicial Branch	Basilosaurus	Mockingbird(s)	Milk	Plantation(s)
Freedmen	Executive Branch		Jefferson Davis	Confederate States of America
State Song	Treaty of Paris of 1763	Woodall Mountain	Climate	Bottlenose Dolphin
Tupelo	Mississippi River	Pinckney's Treaty of 1795	Magnolia	Vicksburg

Mississippi Bingo

Mississippi River	Mockingbird(s)	Territory	Sharecropping (-er)	Judicial Branch
Agricultural	Bottlenose Dolphin	Mississippi Delta	Civil War	Alligator(s)
Jackson	Elvis		Treaty of Paris of 1763	Woodall Mountain
University of Mississippi	State Song	Vicksburg	Pinckney's Treaty of 1795	France/French
Basilosaurus	Fishing	William C. Claiborne	County (-ies)	Tupelo

Mississippi Bingo

Judicial Branch	Territory	Industry (-ies)	Milk	Executive Branch
Native American	Magnolia	Elvis	Fishing	Civil War
Jackson	Treaty of Paris of 1763		France/French	Mississippi River
Climate	Antebellum	State Song	Pinckney's Treaty of 1795	Woodall Mountain
Freedmen	County (-ies)	Sharecropping (-er)	Vicksburg	Tupelo

Mississippi Bingo

Industry (-ies)	William C. Claiborne	Territory	Fishing	Honeybee
State Song	Treaty of Paris of 1763	Mississippi Delta	Woodall Mountain	Alligator(s)
Oprah Winfrey	Vicksburg		Pinckney's Treaty of 1795	Mississippi River
Executive Branch	Border(s)	Mockingbird(s)	Tupelo	Agricultural
County (-ies)	France/French	Judicial Branch	University of Mississippi	Freedmen

Mississippi Bingo

Industry (-ies)	Fishing	University of Mississippi	Territory	Civil War
Honeybee	Judicial Branch	Treaty of Paris of 1763	Milk	France/French
Vicksburg	Confederate States of America		Freedmen	Native American
Union	Executive Branch	Motto	Pinckney's Treaty of 1795	Woodall Mountain
Antebellum	Hurricane Katrina	County (-ies)	Tupelo	State Song

Mississippi Bingo

Judicial Branch	Fishing	Executive Branch	Mississippi Delta	Hurricane Katrina
John J. Pettus	Native American	Mockingbird(s)	Freedmen	University of Mississippi
Jackson	Treaty of Paris of 1763		Alligator(s)	Territory
Honeybee	State Song	Legislative Branch	Pinckney's Treaty of 1795	Woodall Mountain
Civil War	Elvis	Tupelo	Border(s)	Vicksburg

Mississippi Bingo

Cotton	Territory	Milk	Hurricane Katrina	Woodall Mountain
Agricultural	Fishing	Industry (-ies)	France/French	Alligator(s)
Jackson	Jefferson Davis		Freedmen	Mockingbird(s)
Tupelo	Border(s)	Antebellum	Pinckney's Treaty of 1795	Treaty of Paris of 1763
State Song	White-tail Deer	Vicksburg	Judicial Branch	University of Mississippi

Mississippi Bingo: Card No. 30

www.ingramcontent.com/pod-product-compliance
Lightning Source LLC
LaVergne TN
LVHW061341060426
835511LV00014B/2053